What Is Not Understood, Needs to Be Said:

Exploring the Complexities of Black Girls

Dr. Tempest Green Leake

"Who taught you to hate the color of your skin? Who taught you to hate the texture of your hair? Who taught you to hate the shape of your nose and the shape of your lips? Who taught you to hate yourself from the top of your head to the soles of your feet?"

-Malcolm X

Tempest Leake

ISBN: 978-0-578-88039-6

DEDICATION

This is to all my little sisters. I hear you, I see you, and I am you. To my young Black girls that have the spirit and passion to conquer all even though you do not know it yet. Your feathers are coming in, you are gaining your strength, and you are preparing to fly.

What Is Not Understood, Needs to Be Said

FOREWARD

Dr. Tempest Leake's work, *"What is not Understood, Needs to be Said: Exploring the Complexities of Black Girls"* is a book that is genuine in its display of the professional and personal experiences of the author, and her counterparts in the journey of Black girlhood. She identifies the complexities of Black girls as it relates to their hair, their relationships with their parents, relationships with peers, and how they navigate systems that should be in place to nurture and educate them. Dr. Leake displays the Black girls' navigation through life not only through the lens of struggle, but with adaption and triumph. Dr. Leake seeks to educate the reader on how to relate and support Black girls; as well as give power to their unique experiences.

The book gives narration and voice to Black girls that are now educators, health professionals, and human service workers to tell their truths- from the perspective of their past and present. Each complex experience highlighted lends a personal experience of a Black girl. Dr. Leake provides important observations as an assistant principal, dance and step coach, and educator. She also gives unique perspectives to Black girls residing in rural areas.

If you work with, have relationships with, or seek to understand Black girls- this book is a must read.

-Rochelle Huff, LCSW

ACKNOWLEDGMENTS

I have to take the time to acknowledge all of the powerhouse sistas in my life. First, to my courageous little sista's of the I'm A G.I.R.L. Club that started at South Stanly High School, you all have a special place in my heart. To my sistas in education, and sistas in life thank you so much for your testimonials they are beyond powerful. And lastly to my mother, Pamela Ann Green. I love you with all my heart and am forever grateful for the sacrifices you made to make sure I was successful. I hope you will be just as proud of me as I am of you.

PURPOSE

I am here, trapped in my thoughts. Engulfed by my fears and doubts. Afraid that my experience will not be enough to resound with the educational intellectuals of our time. That my words would not be received by those researchers, historians, and other educational gurus that infuse their works with data and studies, but this is not for them. It has become obvious to me that they cannot fix the problem, only shine partial pieces of light on it from sometimes narrow perspectives. We have to take what we have and work towards our solution. I have allowed them to do to me what the world continues to do with Black girls, make them feel inadequate and not accepted.

This book is for anyone raising a young Black girl, teaching young Black girls, or currently existing as a young Black girl. This book is to help bring light to the complexities that come with being born in America, Black and female. As Black girls, we are layered with so many mysteries that those on the outside do not understand, and at times we struggle to understand.

Throughout this work, I will attempt to address some of these complexities and provide guidance to help support our Black girls for those that are attempting to raise and teach them in today's society. There may be some topics in this book that are sensitive and may trigger some. Please know that this work is meant to support and encourage. If you are offended by anything shared, please take time to self-reflect on why that may be occurring.

If you are a mother, read this with your daughter. If you are a counselor, bring a group of girls together and dive into the issues addressed in this book. If you are a mentor, take time to read through and find what will best fit your mentee. If you are an educator, read this in its entirety so that you think before you respond to your Black female students. If you are a father, uncle, brother, or whatever the case may be; take the time to read this to better understand the issues that your daughters, nieces, and sisters face every day that they wake up as a Black female.

Table of Contents

PROLOGUE

For far too long young Black females have been an after-thought in all aspects of society. We have spent centuries in the shadows. There are so many resources, studies, research, and initiatives out there for Black boys. Black girls continue to be left behind. Society and educators are left with the assumption that if they can reach the Black males the Black females will benefit also, but we are not the same. The issues young Black females have to deal with, especially when they cannot shoot a basketball, run a football, or excel in other ways outside of the classroom, can set them back generation after generation. Also when they are not born into privilege we suffer because of our sex and race.

The Condition of Education 2020 study looks at the most current data from the National Center of Education Statistics and is mandated by Congress to aid policymakers in decision-making and to "monitor educational progress". The study reveals that 55% of Black children under 18 are living in a Mother-only household compared to only 17% of white children and 32% of Hispanic children. Of this 55%, 45% are living in poverty. Our Black girls are in a cycle, becoming mothers and trying to raise their children alone and many times depending on assistance to make ends meet. We cannot assume that this is where they want to be, we have to provide ways to get out.

Here is how a senior analyst from the Condition of Education 2020 sums it up:

"Millions of Black parents expect public schools to help their children to be better. Millions of Black students depend on public education to pursue their happiness. We tried hard to find a significant improvement for Black students in the Condition of Education 2020. Yet, what the data demonstrates is disappointing and discouraging. In brief, this annual report mandated by the U.S. Congress suggests that changing the condition of education for Black students needs a true commitment of every policymaker, school leader, and educator."

-Jinghong Cai, Senior Research Analyst

In Washington, D.C., The National Women's Law Center and 20 black girls from the area noted consistent issues with D.C. middle and high school dress codes. The work mentions the exclusion of certain lengths of skirts, and the exclusion of tights, leggings, and headwear. These types of legwear are oftentimes, more affordable and comfortable for growing girls. Also, the need for headbands is growing increasingly popular with the natural hair movement. Who does it hurt to wear a headband or wrap (not bonnet ladies)? The work is called: *"DRESS CODED: Black Girls, Bodies, and Bias in D.C. Schools"*. These simple violations lead to discipline disparities. Monique W. Morris makes it plain in her book *Pushout: The Criminalization of Black Girls in School*. She gives real accounts of girls being criminalized for minor infractions in schools.

In the article, *"A Battle for the Souls of Black Girls"*, it mentions how "Black girls are arguably the most at-risk student group in the United States. But Black girls' discipline rates are not far behind those of Black boys; and in several categories, such as suspensions and law enforcement referrals, the disparities between Black and white girls eclipse those between Black and white boys." *The New York Times'* article dug into the discipline data from the Education Department and discovered "black girls are over five times more likely than white girls to be suspended at least once from school, seven times more likely to receive multiple out-of-school suspensions than white girls and three times more likely to receive referrals to law enforcement."

The study, *Girlhood Interrupted: The Erasure of Black Girls' Childhood*, the authors explore what they call the "adultification" of black girls. Teachers were questioned on aspects of Black female students and white female students across age ranges, and across every range, the teachers viewed Black girls as being more adult than white girls. The age ranges were (0-4), (5-9), (10-14), (15-19). The questions asked the teachers about the girl's independence, how much they needed to be comforted, knowledge about sex, need for support, how often they take on adult responsibilities, and how often do they seem older than their age. Each area in the *"Girlhood Interrupted"* study had Black girls significantly higher, except in the age range 0-4, which shows once Black girls leave pre-k they are seen as more adult than their white female counterparts. This is reflected in the fact that Black girls are more likely to be arrested, suspended, have multiple suspensions, and be referred to juvenile justice at higher rates than white girls.

What we must all understand is that this is not a Black girl problem, this affects us all. We are not setting our Black girls up for success. Are we providing them with all the opportunities that others have? Do we recognize her struggles and strategically start programs, interventions, protocols, and initiatives that target these Black girls to improve their rate of success? Are these actions productive and sustainable? Are you (policymaker, parent, educator, and stakeholder) being intentional in the home, classroom, community, and church to provide activities and opportunities that cater to Black girls? I want to make you aware that these girls are not okay. Yes, they are strong and fierce, but they are still children that need support, guidance, and a fair chance. So we must approach them differently. The following chapters will unlock some of the issues they face and some strategies and resources to address them.

Please approach this with an open-mind, open-heart, and be prepared to reflect on what part you play in a Black girl's life. Are we going to be part of the solution or part of the problem?

What Is Not Understood, Needs to Be Said

1. I Can't Go to School with My Hair like This

Black Hair

For generations, Black females have dealt with scrutiny about our hair. Constantly compared to our non-black counterparts. Our hair, with all of its strength, glory, and uniqueness, is looked down upon in society. There is absolutely no escape from it. Black girls have no control over how their hair comes out of their scalp. Kinky, coiling, wavy, coarse, tight, nappy, 4C, 4B, or whatever you may choose to describe it, it is ours. However, up until recently with the natural hair movement, and the possible links to cancer, Alzheimer's, cysts, and uterine fibroids from the use of relaxers, you would not often see Black women on sitcoms, advertisements, movies, and music videos, or in their everyday lives with their hair in its natural state. Now when you look at Black men, white women, and others, none are asked to wear wigs or straighten their hair or wear their hair in any other state other than what comes out of their scalp, with few exceptions. Why is this? Are we not beautifully packaged as we come?

If you have watched the news or read any recent articles about hairstyle discrimination, then you are aware that many of these hair protocols and "dress codes" that exclude certain hairstyles specifically target who? You guessed it, Black women and Black girls. Hair extensions, braids, short natural styles, big curly hair, and locs have all fallen victim to hair discrimination from the military, schools, and the workplace. I have vivid memories of being picked on because of my hair. I can recall feeling insecure and shrinking myself in school, church, and any place I would be seen.

If you have never paid attention before, see how your Black girl acts when her hair is done versus when it is not. Take notice of the types of hairstyles she gravitates towards. Are they straight (pressed, blowouts, flat irons, relaxers, sew-in-weaves, wigs), locs (dreads, faux locs), braids (crochet, box braids, cornrows), or other natural looks (curls, kinks, afros, puffs, buns)? Allow your Black girl to explore what works for her. What makes her light up and glow? What makes her smile at herself? Let your girl know that no matter the choice she is beautiful. I am not going to argue one way or the other. Being a Black female we should not be placed within any box where we must conform to anyone else's version of ourselves. We do not have the choice of being born female or being born Black, neither of which I want to pose a negative connotation, but we have a choice on how we wish to wear our hair. Allow them to embrace their image and respect all the different types of Black hair.

On my job, I have been asked by white women "Why do you change your hair all the time?" To be completely honest, it is not anyone's business what we do with our hair. Look at R&B star Tamar Braxton and actress and comedian Tiffany Haddish, these women were criticized for cutting their hair short. It's THEIR HAIR. Did you witness the beauty in *Black Panther* as the female warriors wore their bald heads with strength and pride? We have the freedom of wearing our hair however we want. I love exploring different hairstyles and it is one of the things that I have control of. I will always be Black and always be female, but do not try to keep up with my hairstyles. I replied that I like changing up my style because it gives me a sense of control and asked her why she did not change her hairstyle? We will leave the conversation there.

I have witnessed the evolutionary change in young Black girls when they have been allowed to feel beautiful. As an educator, my Black female students were more responsive, engaged, and cheerful in class if they felt their hair was "done". I have seen Black girls become upset, reserved, and defensive if they were trying to mask their edges with a headband and were asked to remove it, or had worn a scarf or bonnet to cover their "unkempt" hair after removing braid or crochets, or even from just the lack of hair care products to take care of it. In my day if we did not have gel, water and, a "Black girl brush" would do. A "Black girl brush" is one that has very close bristles and can catch the nape and the edges to lay your hair down as much as possible to get it in a bun or ponytail.

Due to financial constraints, lack of resources, access to beauticians, and little to no skills with hair, some of our young Black girls find themselves at a disadvantage when it comes to their hair. Today they do have YouTube tutorials, whereas we only had "Black Hair" and "Hype Hair" magazine to refer to for inspiration. There are some key things that young Black girls need in their beauty box: elastic bands (not rubber bands), comb, brush, gel, edge control, hair oil or grease, shampoo, and conditioner. I name these things because schools sometimes provide care bags for female students, but some of these essentials are not included, but are necessary so young Black girls can take care of their hair and feel confident in school. You will find that the key ingredient to young Black female success is building self-esteem and eliminating insecurities.

When I had my hair "done" in school, you could not tell me I wasn't cute because I knew it. I walked on the air created by complements that I would receive. However, when my hair was not "done" I hoped to walk by my peers and get through my day unnoticed. I would raise my hand less, keep my responses short when asked questions, and stare at all the girls (white, Asian, Hispanic) that did not have to worry about hair because it came out of their scalp straight and all they had to do was wash it and put it in a ponytail or let it hang. It did not matter to them that their hair would always be that way, they would maybe dye it, curl it, or cut it shoulder length, and it was still acceptable just hanging there.

It took me years to understand that our hair was powerful. It can do everything their hair can do and more, and it did not have to be washed and shampooed as often to maintain its luster and style. We have to let our young Black girls form a relationship with their hair early and let them know how unique and special their crown is no matter what anyone may have to say or how they decide to wear it. Tiffany Crank, Cancer Program Development Specialist and Dr.PH candidate, age 35, describes her hair journey like this:

"Today I celebrate my 1 year since locing my hair. This may get a little long but I need to say this for anyone that needs to hear it. First, understand this is MUCH bigger than a hairstyle, and it took me a looooong time to get here. For years, I was afraid of wearing my natural hair. Let that sink in...I was afraid to wear my hair how it naturally grew out of my scalp. Afraid of stereotypes. Afraid of looks. Afraid of the assumptions about my personality. Afraid it would negatively affect my career. Afraid of all the super-servings of discrimination that come with looking "too ethnic" in this society. So...assimilated. I straightened and pressed my hair...and chose acceptance. For so many years. I agonized over routine hair appointments. I avoided sweating, inclement weather, pools, and anything else that would mess up my hair at all cost. So much time and energy (and money) went into making sure my hair would look "good" when I stepped out every day. It was physically and mentally EXHAUSTING.

I started thinking about locing my hair about 2 years before I did it. It took me that long to overcome feelings of self-doubt, negative self-image, and to get to that beautiful moment where I realized, you know what-I am me and I DO NOT have to water myself down to make anyone feel more comfortable.

So, this journey is not really about hair. It's about self-acceptance and self-love and feeling confident and beautiful in my skin and kinky roots. I still get the looks. I still feel the assumptions. I still face discrimination. The difference is internal; Honey I smile and flip my hair and keep it moving. This has been the most liberating year of my life, and I have found so much peace, happiness, and confidence within myself. This is why I celebrate today. I hope this encourages anyone facing the same internal battle; be you baby-straight, no chaser."

–Tiffany Crank

So if a young Black girl is in your life in some way, do not sit in judgement if her hair is a little frizzed, but acknowledge her hair and remind her she is beautiful. Also, keep in mind how she may feel because of this. And we cannot exclude her Black female counterparts that will make fun of her because her hair may not be as neat, or well-kept as theirs. This ridicule can be the most detrimental coming from young girls that look like you and whose hair maybe a nappy heap by the end of the week given the moisture outside, or be pulled up into a baby ponytail if she had not just gotten it in braids. So teach your young Black girls to love other young Black girls, so they can be a source of protection and encouragement to each other. They can rise together no matter if their braids are three days old or three weeks old, if her perm (relaxer) is fresh or in need of a touch-up, if her locs are freshly twisted or you cannot see her scalp, and even if her puff is on fleek with edges laid or the shrinkage is real and the kitchen is tight.

Colorism

Relations between Black girls are not always the "sisterhood" that people assume it to be. This is especially true in grades K-12. Black girls can hate each other with such passion, that they cannot stay in the same room together. This self-hate is embedded so deep that there is discrimination among Black girls because of the melanin of their skin. Redbone, brown skin, dark skin, light bright, coco, caramel, and everything in between. Black girls will segregate themselves because of their complexion. I have felt this way as a child. Being selected because I was not "too dark" and being overlooked because I was not "light enough". Being the only Black girl on the cheerleading team. Being jealous that the boys looked at the white girls or the light-skinned girls more than me. Wanting my skin to be lighter and staying out of the sun so I would not get any darker. These are things that plagued my mind as well as the minds of many young Black girls sitting in classrooms and just walking through life not fully loving themselves or appreciating their beauty. What changed my mind was other Black women and Black men (i.e. Resource officers, family, neighbors; not men that were trying to court me) in my life that saw my beauty, intelligence, and strength. The praise I received let me know that my brain was enough, my presence was enough, and I just as I am was enough.

Teachers, white people, and other Black people will also make assumptions about Black girls because of how dark or how light they are. For example, lighter-skinned Black girls are seen as beautiful, smart, and well-behaved. Darker-skinned girls are noted as having bad attitudes, less attractive, and not as intelligent. All of these assumptions are biases that are being portrayed in the media, based on one encounter, or from other people's opinions that have been shared (not from personal experience). Also seeing lighter-skinned women and girls in roles on television, social media, music videos, and all the models you see in the malls can lead darker girls to hate their skin. Now you can mention Lupita N'yongo, Naomi Campbell, and Aja Naomi King, but there is not a laundry list of them out there or that are recognized as they should be.

I have heard young Black men, my students, those I have helped, coached, and mentored speak about how light-skinned girls and dark-skinned - girls act differently. Some young Black men have placed Black girls into a box and look at them through generalizations and stereotypes. They tell me Black girls have bad attitudes, "they are too loud", they are always in drama, they try to tell us what to do, "I don't need another mama", which is what these young men say. I respond by asking them to look deeper. If you will not date Black girls or darker-skinned - girls because of these things, are you telling me that your mom, sister, aunts are all this way, and future daughter will be this way as well? Do you not want a woman that has an opinion or one who can speak her mind? Or do you prefer someone that caters to your needs and agrees with everything you say? Girls look out for these types of guys, they are not ready for you yet. Give them time, love yourself, and know that you are beautiful.

There have been many works that have addressed the more pleasing aesthetic as being that which is closest to our blonde hair, blue-eyed counterparts when it comes to measuring beauty. This means you must have fair skin and "good hair" to be attractive. Now fair skin can be a blessing and a curse. We cannot ignore the fact that these young Black girls can easily fall victim to advances by clergy, family members, men in the streets, and other unwanted attention that is not to a fault of her own. This "beauty" can come with a price that these girls have to carry for the rest of their lives. This can be remedied if we continue to encourage and educate our daughters, sisters, cousins, students, nieces, whatever they are to you; that their Black is beautiful and that at the end of the day...Black is Black. Some light-skinned girls may learn this the hard way through experience that no matter how light you are, in the eyes of others you are still Black. What we as Black girls and Black women must realize is that until we come together as a united front this battle amongst ourselves will continue to hold us back.

I have seen, heard testimony, and read of lighter-skinned girls being jumped, having their hair cut, faces scarred, and being ostracized just for "thinking she is cute" or "she thinks she is better than us" when that could not be further from the truth. And in contrast, darker-skinned girls, called "Blacky", "midnight", "tar baby" and a host of other things that bring them to tears and make them hate themselves to the point of wanting to take their lives, bleach their skin, and straighten their hair. Young Black girls have been asked, "Is your skin dark because you drank too much chocolate milk or coffee?" Asked "does the color rub off?" Mrs. McClendon, M.Ed., middle school ELA teacher, reflects on her first experience with colorism in elementary school, with an incident to some that can seem so subtle, but to this young Black girl, it was so much more at the time and still is today.

"I remember when I was in 5th grade at Wingate Elementary School. It was a place where I knew that I was loved by my teachers, a place where I knew that they truly wanted the best for me. I didn't see racism until that cold rainy day. Getting ready for school I remember my mom telling me that I needed my gloves and my coat, and to make sure that I brought them home. Now these gloves that I had, girl let me tell you that they were

AMAZING! They were all Black with fur around them. And they fit my hand perfectly. These gloves gave me life!!!!!!

It was after school when I realized that my amazing gloves were missing. I looked all through my book bag, in my coat pocket and they were not there. I was getting nervous. Various scenes were playing through my mind about how my mom would react. Would she yell at me? Would she give me a whopping? Will she give me that disappointing look that would pierce my soul? (Yes, my mom had that death stare!)

Then I heard someone, one of my white classmates call my name, "Alecia, are these your gloves?" I replied with an ecstatic yes! I told her thank you, and she gave them to me. While I was excited that she found my gloves, and relieved that the scenes that played through my mind were a distant memory, I remembered how she was holding them.

She was holding the AMAZING black gloves that gave me life as if she was holding up a dead animal, as if they were dirty like my gloves weren't too good for her. And when she gave them to me, she wiped her hands on her pants as if she was wiping off "my blackness." I was as confused as to why she did this. She was someone who I would talk to during lunch and played with during recess. I began looking at my gloves to see if they were dirty. I smelled them to make sure that they smelled fresh. These gloves were brand new, these gloves were AMAZING, these gloves gave me life, or at least I thought they did. But why would she do that to me?

When I got home, I told my mom what happened. And that's when we had "the talk". She told me the color of my skin, while it's beautiful, rich, powerful, strong, and unique. There will be people who will look at you and see dirt but that doesn't mean that you are It means that people look at you and they don't see your worth. They will mistreat you and try to tear you down. But you don't let them. You always remember who you are, and where you come from. And don't let anyone tell you that you are dirty. You are fearfully and wonderfully made, and what you have inside of you nobody can take that away from you.

I'm 39 years old now, and that memory is still with me. That memory still hurts to this day. But something beautiful came out of that memory, it was my mother reminding me of who I am. How I am a rich, powerful, strong, and unique BLACK WOMAN who continues to push boundaries every single day."

-Alecia McClendon

We have to do better for our girls in society, but it begins at home and school. Parents, teachers, and others need to expose the girls to their reflection. They need to see art, movies, literature, and other women in their lives that look like them. Things that showcase their beauty in a positive light. They need role models that look like them and share the experience that they have endured. This may not always seem that simple, but we have to make the effort to make it happen. This may make you have to go outside of your comfort zone, but it is worth the effort.

Parents of students that are not of color need to educate their children on how to be inclusive, letting them know that we are all different, but still the same. Our feelings get hurt just like theirs, we are all human and have emotions. Teach them acceptance and how to appreciate how God made us. Not just tolerance, we do not want to be tolerated, we want to be treated with dignity and respect.

Resources could be at church with a youth group or minister, school, a black woman in law enforcement, local politicians, or the local NAACP. If you live near a college or community college campus inquire about any of their teams or organizations that may be willing to do some volunteer work. For younger girls, see if there are high school girls or athletic teams that do not mind being mentors. I know women that are not "of color" can be positive resources as well, but I have found that the difference is made deeper and long-term if the person looks like them. Remember it is about the reflection they see that can change their mindset.

Body Image

We see images of little girls wearing their mother's heels, playing in her makeup, and trying out her jewelry. These things are cute and normal in most cases for little girls. However, in today's society with the pressure to have the biggest booty, the nicest curves, and a flawless face, Black girls may reduce themselves to just a body. No thoughts, no opinions, no respect, and no modesty. Do not get me wrong, I have taught dance, step, and modeling and have been known for the occasional twerk, which you may see something wrong with, but it has its place.

So before I proceed, let me clear this up so that you do not think I am granting any young girl permission to parade around on social media or YouTube twerking. I am talking fully clothed organized dancing they may involve the booty. What everyone must understand is that we as Black people have traditional dances linked to our African roots that involve the movement of the hips and what some would consider looking "twerk-like". These dances are used in religious and spiritual rituals, weddings, social gatherings, and also to show strength and unity. If you have been educated at a Historically Black College, seen an HBCU band perform, or seen their cheerleader's battle, you know that these movements are not foreign in our culture, it is art, it takes great strength, endurance, and talent (rhythm) to accomplish. Moving your booty just for attention sake is not what I am referring to, and to be completely honest the white girls are out there twerking just as much if not more than we are. I am very proud of my heritage and admire the traditions of my ancestors.

What Is Not Understood, Needs to Be Said

To refocus, Black girls have historically reached puberty before their white counterparts, and just to add this is true for Hispanic girls as well. This means the development of our female features at an earlier age, breast, hips, thighs, butt, and beginning our menstrual cycle. I do not have to tell you how many times I have had students that surpassed me in both height and curves. During trips, games, college tours, and any activity that involved the opposite sex, and sometimes that did not matter either, I had to protect my Black girls from stares, comments, and wandering hands. Just because a girl looks like a woman does not mean her mind is that of a woman, and to be honest this is a tough combination for our young Black girls who need love and attention. Developing early causes a host of issues that we need to be prepared to address at all levels: at home, at school, on social media, and in society.

This topic of body image can be a double-edged sword. Some girls embrace their curves, while some girls hate and hide their curves. Some young Black girls can be made to feel very insecure about themselves. This causes these young Black girls to make themselves shrink. I will refer to shrinking throughout the book. By shrinking I mean placing themselves into a bubble where they feel they are not seen or heard. They do not allow their light to shine. They will not talk or engage in any way, they lose their voice. Society and the adults they have encountered have slowly chipped away at their self-esteem until they become a smaller version of themselves. In comes doubt, fear, anxiety, and a decrease in self-worth.

Some girls believe that their curves make them even more unattractive. So they figure they have to find another way to magnify other assets that they have. Well, I'm not attractive, so I have to be smart. I'm not attractive, so make sure that my clothes are always really neat and clean. I'm not attractive, so I got to be a great athlete or I will be the class clown, if they are laughing with me then they will not laugh at me.

They make themselves compensate in other ways because they feel as though they have to be able to find positive attention in another way. Sometimes it can lead to them being a bully. And to be completely transparent other negative ways to get attention can be resorted to such as having sex or being what boys call "easy". These are all unfortunate issues that our Black girls deal with daily, unless there is someone in their lives providing a positive light or something offered as a positive outlet, for them to gain a positive view of themselves.

In some cases, our young Black girls can begin to self-hate. Hate their weight, their skin, hate who they *think* they are. Keep in mind, I am not directing this towards being overweight, it could be girls that are naturally small as well. Starving themselves or overeating to cope with the pain of their insecurities about their body can seem like the easiest thing to do without support and encouragement. We have also had issues with our young Black girls cutting themselves as well, which will be addressed in a later chapter.

Some young Black girls do not like the attention they get because of their body, so they decide to cover up with baggy clothes. Because they do not want that uncle, cousin, drunk friend, or neighbor to get the wrong idea. They find themselves in a situation where they have to protect themselves from something they should not have to worry about. We have to make sure that we are the ones protecting them.

At home, we must instill in our young Black girls what comes with the changes in her body. Encourage her that these changes are nothing to be ashamed of, but also nothing to play with. She has to know to respect herself and to command respect from others. We have to teach our girls that their bodies are just that...theirs. No one has the right to make them feel objectified, less than, feel as though they are grown, insecure, or other. No one man, woman, boy, or girl has the right to touch them in a way that makes them feel uncomfortable. Also, share how to wear clothes in a way that does not make them feel ashamed or self-conscious.

At school, I always share with my girls when they wear clothes that are deemed inappropriate that what they have on in some cases is cute, but it is my job to protect them from unwanted advances. And in turn teach whoever comes at them the wrong way that just because a girl dresses a certain way does not give them an open invitation to touch, grab, or say anything to them that is inappropriate. I tell my girls "know what they are going out looking for, dress accordingly, and that is what you will attract". I spent many years being one of the guys wearing baggy clothes, and many years trying to regain my girlhood.

With the limited resources that some of our girls have, do not be quick to judge what she is wearing. You may not know that she is wearing hand-me-downs and has a parent at home doing the best they can. Ask the right questions, or find out the "why" before you openly chastise a child for being out of the dress code. Also, do not ignore the skinny white girl with no butt to walk around in Soffe shorts and send the Black girl with the "ghetto booty" to me for wearing the same shorts. Do you expect her to wear big gym shorts, further pointing out the fact that she is well endowed and deepening her into her insecurities? Stop pointing out the young lady that has developed her curves sooner than others because it makes her feel uncomfortable or inadequate. If you cannot have the proper conversation with her, and this is a sensitive one, find someone who can, but do not risk the relationship you could form by singling her out.

Talk to your young Black girls about the dangers of social media, sexting, and child pornography. Displaying your body in these ways can have long-standing consequences. This could prevent them from gaining access to colleges, jobs, and opportunities that could project them into successful situations. Make them aware that there is no way to ensure that these images and video can be deleted and not shared, and can come back to haunt them in the form of blackmail. I have seen little boys use this to hold girls hostage in bad relationships, older men use this to keep girls from telling on them, and other girls bully them with threats to expose them. This is happening all around us and our girls are falling victim to these types of harassment and don't have a way out. We have to teach them that there are people that care and there is a way out. Here is what Shonta, age 31, has to say about her journey with body image:

"Being too heavy or slightly overweight was something that affected me as a young child and the fact that I am a Black girl did not make things any better. Can you imagine, being a little girl who already has to worry about not being the right color to play a specific role in a play but also having to worry about being the right size as well? Growing up I was the one friend who developed way earlier than other girls my age, especially much faster than my White, Asian, and Chinese classmates.

What Is Not Understood, Needs to Be Said

I can remember being in the 7th grade, running up against a white classmate who was just as popular as myself, for a part in a big musical play for the school. However, she was much slimmer than I was and had beautiful long blonde hair and bright blue eyes with the cutest small feet; while I had short curly black hair, stood 3 ½ inches taller than her and at least 25 pounds heavier wearing a size 9 shoe. Even though I knew as well as everyone else that I had this part in the bag, somehow, I was not good enough to play the part because even after winning the vote of my peers; I did not win the final vote from the music teacher. Ultimately, I felt as though I was not the right size and just maybe they thought someone smaller would be a better fit for the part. Although I did not let that obstacle stop me from trying out for other activities, it did however hurt my pride.

I found myself carrying around this thought in my head of never being good enough because I was not the perfect size for the part. Watching what I ate and not eating as much became a habit for me because there was no way I was letting my size hinder me from accomplishing any of my goals throughout life. I could not let the fact that I am a Black girl who just so happens to be an early bloomer define me. In doing this it caused me to become more focused on my appearance and how thinner I looked more than how my grades (which had begun to drop). I no longer cared what the teacher was talking about during class, but was more worried about how small my jeans made me look or if the color of my shirt made me look too fat. Soon after trouble followed because I started feeling as though, no matter what I did I would never be good enough!

Soon after, I gained inspiration about my size and use it to my advantage by becoming an awesome athlete. One sport happened to be football! I ended up trying out for football and to my surprise, I made the cut! Knowing the odds were already against me because the color of my skin made it more worst looking as if I were an 18-year-old trapped in the body of a middle schooler. So, I took all the determination and will power I had in me and became one of the greatest players on the team. With that, I built my self-esteem and continued to drive myself to be excellent not only in sports but in academics as well.

Throughout the years I've managed to carry my weight with courage and knowing that no matter how my body is shaped or how I appear to look on the outside, I was and always will be good enough for anything that I set my mind to. I hope to inspire the next Black girl who may have a slightly bigger stomach, much wider hips, extremely longer feet to never let her body image stop or come in between her and greatness! We as Black girls may not come in the perfect shape or even be fit for the part in a school play, but we can do or be anything that we put our minds to no matter our size or even the color of our skin.

-Shonta Davis "Bam"

Body image does not stop at a Black girl's figure developing at an early age. As women of

African descent, we also deal with our facial features be more pronounced than other races. Our lips are very full and prominent on our faces and our noses, though they can vary in size, are usually more broad and full. I for one dealt with being picked on because my lips were "big" according to some of my peers. So, similar to other cases, I have seen young Black girls do things to cover their faces or shy away from certain makeup that would draw attention to their features. I have seen young Black girls cover their mouths when they speak, suck their thumb, tuck their lips, and refrain from wearing lipstick or colored gloss for fear it would make their lips look bigger. I have had numerous conversations with Black teenage girls that wish their noses were narrower, smaller, and less noticeable. Here again, we have to instill self-love.

Share with our daughters that these are the features of our ancestors, and take notice of how they look like their mom or dad. Also, look at how others pay money for injections into their lips and fix their noses. Cosmetic lines have glosses, lipsticks, and other items they sell to enhance the look of lips and make them look more "plumper". Black girls...people pay good money to look like you. They go to the tanning bed and lay out in the sun to give themselves more color. You are what others aspire to be. Do not be ashamed of all that you have been given.

We have to teach our young Black girls to love themselves inside first. Once you convince them that they are valuable and what is outside is just a bonus, they begin to become the woman they were destined to be. Learning that their value comes from within, what is in their hearts and minds is what matters most.

2. Mommy and Daddy Issues

The presence of parents is vital to young Black girls forming their identity. It is the foundation of what healthy relationships should look like, what family looks like and determines the support that Black girls will have throughout their school years and their lives. The family structures that our young Black girls grow up in vary widely and have a major effect on which way the needle will tilt. Throughout my 36 years of living and 14 years in education, I have seen everything you can think of when it comes to the family structure and raising of Black girls. Now you may say well all girls go through these different structures that I mention, but keep in mind the generational consistency that affects our Black girls, dating back to slavery. These structures are deeply rooted and we are fighting them every day.

Recall our ancestors who were not allowed to marry, or whose marriages were not recognized by whites. Also the removal of babies that were born of our slave four-mothers and sold as property. The consistent buying, selling, and trading of members of slave families as if there were no connections, bonds, love. The raping of slave women by their masters and their babies not being fully aware of their identity. The struggle that women as a whole have had to overcome throughout history to gain their rights to an education, to work in other functions other than house labor, their right to vote, and to be recognized as full citizens. We are still fighting for gender equality today. We have to make our young Black girls aware of this fight that the odds are stacked against them, but they can be equipped with the weapons they need to fight the generational curses that come along with being Black and female.

"I hate my mom!" Words that I could not fathom because my mother was such as essential part of my life, but this statement was familiar with many young girls I taught. Now, this of course caught me off guard because there is almost a consensus in the Black community that the mother, the strong Black woman, the way maker, is the backbone of the Black family. In many instances this is 110% true, however, in the case of some of my girls, this is far from the truth. Look at the movie "Precious", the mental and physical abuse that can come from a mother who has been a product of these same scars. These things are happening all around us. We have young mothers that are not prepared to take on the task and their daughters become their friends and when the daughter is ready to be raised it is usually too late to get her on the right path without the right supports in place.

Some of our Black mothers leave their children to be raised by their mothers, so they can reclaim their glory days. They look at their daughters as what they use to be or what they could have been and begin to resent them. They blame them for why they have lost their figure, yell at them when they get looks from men (instead of putting those men in their place), and leave them to fend for themselves with the guidance of their grandmother, who may be too many generations behind to keep up with a blooming teenager and social media.

You also have the addicted mother. The mother is addicted to drugs, alcohol, sex, bad relationships, having babies, drama, etc. This mother can neglect the basic needs of her daughter in an effort to fulfill her lust. This mother will spend the rent money or the light bill money. She may also sell her food stamps for cash to feed her addiction. She may be in the home, but may not be present. At times she blames her daughter(s) for her problems, which can lead to verbal and physical abuse that will be talked about more extensively in a later chapter. This revolving door and inconsistency that daughters see are all a mosaic of bricks that create the wall that she has up. This wall can prevent her from learning in the classroom, from forming positive relationships with women, and creating an attitude for life that is resentful and hurt.

One thing we must realize is that for every year it took to create this wall it can take that long to fully break it down. Girls that have endured this type of trauma often feel alone, unloved, have abandonment issues, are angry, frustrated, and will give you the business if you cross them the wrong way. These girls have to be handled with care, we have to prevent them from going down the same paths their mothers travelled.

We must open their eyes to opportunities, experiences, and positive relationships that can instill hope and empower them to see past the hurt and anger. Introduce them to mentors, therapists, guidance counselors, support groups, sports, hobbies, writing, dancing. These outlets can contribute to their healing process.

In my case, and the cases of many other young Black girls, I grew up with a very supportive, hardworking mother, but my father was not present. I watched my mother walk to work in all types of weather to provide for us until she got herself in a better position. In instances like this, there is only so much a mother can do. And though many young ladies that have a present mother appear to be fine and can still function and live successful lives, the absence of a father can have long-term effects. The presence of a father, a "good" father, in particular, sets precedence for some of the unconscious layers of a girl that are not always at the forefront of our minds. One, a girl's first love, a daddy's love, can correlate with a young girl's self-esteem. The attention, encouragement, and push of a male figure can bring a different sense of self in a female. This creates more confidence and can offer different perspectives to a certain situation that females may handle differently.

Two, relationships, I know Black women that have spent their lives, including myself, trying to find a man who was just like their father or the complete opposite. The relationship your father has with you can correlate with the types of boyfriends Black girls choose, the level of standards they have for long-term relationships, and whether they are interested in men at all. I have spoken with girls that have chosen to be homosexual because of the relationship their dad has with their mom or because of the abuse they have suffered from their father. I am not saying this is the case for all decisions on sexuality at all, however, these are true accounts I have heard from friends and students I have taught. Some young Black girls have witnessed their mother's be physically and mentally abused and they begin to believe that this is how a man shows love, and in response will allow their boyfriends to abuse them in the same way, confusing the abuse with love.

Third, there is the complete absence of a father. This lack of relationship can cause resentment, anger, distrust, and dependency from the wrong man. For the father that misses Christmas', birthdays, proms, graduations, and athletic events, these things can be detrimental to a young Black girl's success and begin to reduce her identity. A child's identity is a combination of that of both parents, when one is absent, young girls can fill that void with something less desirable or push themselves to be beyond perfect to compensate for not being complete.

Some fathers decide that being a father is not what they had planned and bailout, leaving innocent little girls with questions that will never be answered. Some fathers get caught up in the criminal justice system and can only be seen through a glass, heard from through a collect call, or written to in letters with a child waiting for advice or guidance that they may need right away. Some mothers can fall into this category as well.

Adults all have circumstances in their lives that cannot be undone, but they have to hold themselves responsible for the human beings they bring into the world. We do have fathers that stay, work hard but are still not "present" for their daughters. Young Black girls need to see a man as more than just a financial provider. You have to feed into them emotionally as well. This can spark what your daughter needs to thrive on her own.

I have continued to battle with the absence of my father in my life. He lived less than twenty minutes away from me and months and years could pass without me seeing him. His inconsistency, lack of communication, and loveless presence have been a constant pain in my heart. As a child you blame yourself, you sit by the door or look out the window at every passing car waiting for him to arrive, and wonder why he doesn't care enough to show up. The yearning for his approval of how well you played at your game, how excellent your grades are, how beautiful you look at prom mounts into a heap of sadness that takes years to overcome. Fathers, your young Black daughter needs you, not just financially, but she needs you to be physically and emotionally present. Give her the courage she needs to leave that abusive relationship, the confidence to make that A or B on her test, and the compliments when she changes her hair or outfit as she leaves the house for school. She also needs you to admonish her when she is wrong, explain to her why, and show her the right way. She needs to know that if no other man on Earth ever loves her you   do.

3. They Don't Know What You <u>Won't</u> Tell Them

In my early days as a teacher I discovered that many Black mothers and guardians were not discussing uncomfortable topics with their young Black girls. I was alarmed by how many girls had not discussed issues that plague Black women and even the basic fundamental information that all girls need to know about their changing bodies. Why do we wait until she gets her period to discuss what it is? Why do we condemn our girls for pregnancy when we have not discussed contraceptives and birth control? Why do our girls have to wait for the

P.E. teachers to introduce them to the wonderful world of Sexually Transmitted Diseases (STDs)? Our Black girls need to know that Heart Disease, Cancer, Stroke, Diabetes, and Alzheimer's Disease are the top five leading causes of death in African American women according to the CDC (Center for Disease Control).

I partnered with our local Department of Social Services to bring these issues to young Black girls (with parental permission) in a more intimate setting where they were free to ask questions without judgement or the "look" that we sometimes give young Black girls when they ask something we may not be comfortable discussing or are prejudging and wondering why they want to know.

Making young Black girls aware of the way their bodies work and why certain anatomical things are happening is essential. How to protect themselves from disease and pregnancy are essential to their self-awareness. They need to know that there are options and that abstaining from sexual activity is the ultimate way to protect themselves from these things. They need to know that some of these sexually transmitted diseases cannot be cured such as HIV (AIDS), Herpes, and Human Papillomavirus (HPV), which now has a prevention treatment available. Some STDs have little to no signs or symptoms so you or your partner could be spreading this and not know it. You will be surprised how exploring these topics will make them think twice.

Black girls start to question how boys have it so much easier and can begin to value their bodies, which can lead to them having more self-respect and being willing to preserve it or be more particular about how they share their bodies. Feminine hygiene can be discussed and the importance of cotton in your wardrobe when it comes to underwear, as well as tight-fitting clothes, bathing/grooming routines, dental hygiene, and how deodorant (aluminum-free if possible) is your friend. This will make you confident being around others and make you easier to be around. I have had to de-escalate many fights and arguments due to someone smelling like "fish" or "onions"...and to be honest, more than half the time it was very true. But it is important for us as parents, educators, guardians, and mentors to educate on the importance of taking care of our bodies.

This leads to self-care. Many people in general are already at a disadvantage for finding positive ways to cope. Add being Black and female to the mix and you have a whole mess on your hands. The stereotypes that follow Black women do not magically appear when a Black girl turns 18, no ma'am. Young Black girls get labeled as being angry, having bad attitudes, being hard to deal with, and in contrast still having to be placed in the "Strong Black Woman" category when she is just a little girl. Just because we are born into this sisterhood does not mean we acquire all these things at birth. Life brings on these attributes that are sometimes only mirrors of our mothers, grandmas, aunts, and sisters. So, because of this label of being strong, many times girls assume the position and do not know how to positively deal with their stress, emotions, and overall mental health.

We, as Black women/girls, have not been traditionally taught to seek a therapist, psychologist, or counselor when we are faced with adversity. We tighten our bootstraps and bury it deep inside until it explodes on that educator, a peer in school, or our parents and loved ones at home. Mental health issues are real and going untreated and undiagnosed will transcend beyond the lifetime of that young Black girl, it can create generations and generations of untreated mental health. I have taught and encountered girls in my career and personal life that in my heart I know were suffering from various mental illnesses.

Bipolar disorder, Mania, Depression, Anxiety, Panic Disorder, and Post-Traumatic Stress Disorder (PTSD) is just a shortlist of issues that run ramped in our community and our Black girls are left to fend for themselves. Without proper medical care from a therapist, psychiatrist, and counselor and in some cases medication, these health issues can cause serious damage. If left untreated, our young girls may hurt themselves by cutting their arms and legs (sometimes in places we may not see right away), starving themselves (Anorexia Nervosa), over-eating (Bulimia), engaging in early sexual activity, or fighting. These harmful actions can lead to young Black girls being hospitalized, suspended, criminalized, or even worse...dying. Some just spend all their lives making others miserable or just hating themselves.

Now some young Black girls have learned to suppress their feelings and go on to lead seemingly normal lives until their past comes back to haunt them and it becomes too much to bear. Individuals that suffer from these mental illnesses and disorders live successful lives managing these areas with therapy and medication.

I am fully aware that in the Black community we turn to God for healing and deliverance from issues in life, however, the God I serve gives us the sense to know when and how to seek medical attention. He has blessed individuals with the appropriate skills to help young people manage mental health illnesses and doctors and scientists with the ability to create medicines to target the symptoms of these disorders. We have to give them a chance.

We, as a community, need to address this head-on in our homes, schools, churches, jobs, and communities. We will overlook issues because we think it is not our place to address them, but the conversation has to start somewhere, why not with you? Many school systems now offer mental health therapists, social workers, guidance counselors, resource officers, and behavior management techs that can help address these needs and point you in the right direction of the resources needed to help young Black girls with these issues early. I am aware of the waitlist, improper placement (the wrong person treating the patient), and difficulty of locating the resource due to your geographic area, but do not continue to allow these obstacles to prevent you from helping your young Black girl. The payoff is worth the initial struggle.

Self-care, if taught at a young age, can save so many young Black girls and help them to become productive, lucid, peaceful young Black women. Many things can be introduced to our girls that require little to no money and minimal resources. Some of the free alternatives include introducing them to yoga, journaling, breathing techniques, and meditation. This can help with decreasing stress, anxiety, blood pressure, and aid with aggression and anger. I am not an expert on these things but there are plenty of certified professionals that share videos online and on YouTube that can give you strategies and visual examples of how to introduce and execute these things. Have your daughter start a hobby, does she like to sing, dance, poetry, gaming, coding, or creating a blog? Sometimes it can start just taking her out for a walk. Some girls are great at creating things and may have a hidden talent like doing hair, makeup, or lashes and brows.

Invest in these outlets for her. Allow your Black girl to explore her creative side.

4. "I am too young for this!"

Have you ever had to watch three or four younger siblings? Not just babysitting for an hour or two. I am talking from the morning you wake up you are giving baths, if there is water, and getting everyone's clothes and book bags on. Cooking breakfast, if there happens to be food in the house that morning, and walking them to school or the bus. This is followed by getting yourself ready for school, making sure your chores are done, homework is complete, and you get to school on time. Once at school you are tired, worried if you signed your little brother's paper, and wondering what you will feed everyone when you get home this evening.

Many of our young Black girls are faced with these adult stresses in middle and high school. They spend their childhood being a mother to someone else's children and start to believe they are grown and that it is their responsibility to care for the younger ones. Will the lights be on? Did he/she make sure the rent was paid? Do I need to call grandma again to get the kids (brothers and sisters not your kids) off the bus? If the baby girl gets sick I will have to sacrifice and stay home, I already have too many absences...What does a child do? The thought of this overwhelms me, imagine taking this on when you do not truly have the means to answer or fix these problems. And we expect these children to enter school and society and be able to function like normal students and citizens, if normal exists.

High school Black girls may even have a job to help support their families and make up for the losses. They are juggling bills, buying food, and contemplating what is important. "Should I just drop out of school and work full time?" Once they get to this point some cannot see a quick means to an end so they do what is easier, quit school, work a minimum wage job that is equally stressful, and try to maintain a household that is not theirs to maintain and once again she will be fighting her way out of a hole.

The hurt and stress of having to be an adult when you are just a teenager is real. Now in some cases, the mother/father may be working and is just trying to make ends meet, while in others the adult may be dealing with their vices and maybe was too young to be a parent. So while we can't sit and place blame and make excuses for the situation, what should we be doing to help these young Black girls dealing with this scenario? We have to start asking the right questions, performing home visits, get out of our heads that this is not our business. The success of these young women is all of our business. Unless there is a relationship formed, you may never get the information you need.

Make yourself aware of changes in behavior, performance, attendance. Making that phone call to the school, counselor, Department of Social Services, etc. can be the first step to not just saving her from drowning in early adulthood, but also save the younger children from the same fate.

I am not saying that watching siblings is a bad thing, I had to do it and it teaches responsibility and other valuable lessons about accountability, however, children should not be the primary caregiver to children.

Also, keep in mind that this girl may have her defenses up, she may cover for that parent, be afraid she will get in trouble, or even worse lose her siblings during a foster care split. She may not quickly volunteer this information and even think that she has it under control. So do not try to take this on by yourself, refer her to a counselor, social worker, mental health therapist, or other health professionals that can help her with this problem. We are not all equipped to handle these situations, and even I know when something is out of my league and I must seek out someone that is trained to help.

Digging deeper into this situation, some girls find themselves seeking an escape from the stress and may turn to a boyfriend or girlfriend for support. What happens if she becomes pregnant? Also, the need for stress relief can turn to dependency on drugs or alcohol, leaving the kids to fend for themselves again. Cycles like these must be stopped.

Parents and guardians, first and foremost, must be held accountable. Take responsibility for your children and if you cannot, there are good families out there that are willing to love your children. Seek out family members that can help you temporarily until you can get on your feet. And we preach about it taking a village to raise a child and turn a blind eye to these situations. "She should not have had all of those kids," they say. Well at this point it is too late for that conversation, the kids are here what can the village do to help? We have to be all in to take our girls to the next level. It may not be easy, and nothing is fixed overnight, but our girls are worth it. Our future is worth it. We do not want that 55% of Black mother-only households to continue and with them living in poverty. Again, break the cycle.

5. The Silent Black Girl, Don't Let Them Shrink

Loud, angry, bad attitude, disrespectful Black girls. "Why is it always the Black girls?" they say. Well, it seems that the only Black girls that get the attention are the ones that are acting out. Many of us are reserved, quiet, humble, and hidden. We fade into the background, hoping not to get called on or called out. But, just because a Black girl isn't disrupting your class or your life, does not mean that she is invisible and should be ignored. This young Black girl does have a voice and it deserves to be heard, but she is waiting for someone, anyone to ask the right questions. This Black girl can be an excellent student, but be harboring massive burdens and still not reach her full potential.

She may fly under the radar and miss out on being identified as Academically Gifted, scholarship opportunities, college recommendations, and not have the support to navigate her way through high school and college. Without proper support, she may not get that opportunity to take the AP courses, miss the deadline for SATs, not know how to apply for waivers for college admissions applications, and be unaware of the credits needed to even apply.

She sits quietly waiting for class to be over and you have no idea what she has to go home to. So she continues to passively sit in class, migrating from one grade to the next, she is a good girl, but not good enough for you to acknowledge her, to help her, so long as she is not a behavior issue and she can perform well for you on her state exam. Just a number at the end of the term. Or she is no trouble at home, does all of her chores, and stays out of your way. We need you to make her your problem. Ask her how she is doing, what does she aspire to be, does she have questions about how she plans to get there, what are her interest or hobbies? She is waiting on you to initiate the conversation.

Parents if your daughter is existing in silence ask why, look for signs, clues, and changes in her behavior. The silence can be a cry for help. We cannot assume that because she is not vocalizing her thoughts and feelings that she is okay. Have you talked to her? Do you speak regularly about, school, their future, or just how their day went? Silent girls could be dealing with self-esteem issues, depression, bullying, or possibly an academic issue that has not surfaced because she is not having a behavior issue.

Recall back to when you were in high school or middle school. Can you even remember the names of some of the Black girls in your class? The silent ones, the ones that did not act out, the ones that may not have been the most beautiful? The ones that were more calm and reserved, barely spoke? The ones that would change clothes in the stall for gym instead of changing with the rest of the girls by the lockers. The ones that wear oversized clothes, no makeup, hair pulled back, just plain and simple. Can you remember her name? Do you know where she is now? Are you friends on social media? Or was she left to fend for herself because no teacher, student, parent, or friend took the time to care?

These young Black girls go through different traumas and abuse that may go unnoticed because they wear it so well, they do not share it with anyone and no one takes the time to ask. You have to make sure that you are making an honest effort with all the young Black girls in your life or that cross your path and find a way to acknowledge the silence.

Everyone is going through something. Take the time out to hold that young Black girl after class and engage in conversation with her. Parents, make that extra effort to probe your daughters with questions to get her to open up about what may be going on. Because she is looking for help from someone, but whether she finds it or not depends on us.

Now some girls are not as quiet, but they do wear a facade. They put on a smile in school in front of their peers to make everyone believe that everything is okay. They even go as far as to encourage other young Black girls on what they should be doing with their lives. And how they can be doing better, how to become more successful in the classroom, on a sports team, or just in life in general...when their lives are on fire around them as we speak.

And sometimes our Black girls put on the same smile at home with the parents making them believe that everything at school is okay. But they are afraid to even go to school. They are afraid to change classes. They are afraid of what the boys will say and do and equally afraid of the girls. They do not believe that their teachers like them. And they carry this with them all the time.

How do we help them? How do we advocate for them? The first thing is not to ignore it. A lot of the suggestions in this book are not just for a specific chapter, but they are interchangeable and can be used throughout different situations that have and will be addressed. We have to make sure that we are not ignoring the signs the symptoms the behaviors suggest, so that none of our Black girls get left behind. Mrs. McDowell, M.Ed., middle school math teacher (working on administrative license), shares her powerful story about her educational journey:

"As I take a look back at my journey at how I got here, I try to remember what it was like for me during my K-12 years. I don't remember much, I can remember a teacher's face but not any names. I can also remember every school I attended which was much more than I probably should have but of course, I didn't know that at the time. I would sometimes move from a school and then back to a school in the same year. I was what they called academically gifted and was often the only Black child in the room. I was a quiet student who did nothing all year. I never opened a book, did homework, or studied, but always seemed to do well on the test.

My most vivid memory of a teacher was when I was in middle school. I sat in the back of doing nothing and the principal asked why I wasn't doing anything, the teacher responded, don't worry she always does well on the test. Fast-forward to high school 11th grade, I just sort of disappeared. I got a job at the local beauty supply store and as a got more hours, I attended school less. Nobody noticed, nobody called. I eventually stop going altogether.

Later I went to the community college thinking I should get my GED. The guy that owned the beauty supply store said I was too smart to be working there and told me if I got my GED he would let me keep my same hours and leave early to go to night school. When I spoke to the admission officers they told me I only needed 2 credits to receive my high school diploma. Of course, I thought she was mistaken. There's no way I was allowed to drop out of school for 2 credits. I went on to finish those two credits and that's where I met my first teacher. He lived in the neighborhood I walked through to get home and said to me every day I walked past him, I'll see you next semester. I thought yeah right, and he did see me next semester.

I signed up for community college and later went on to join the military where I served 13 years. While in the military I earned a Master's degree in education. This brings me to where I am today. Education changed my life, knowing the importance of education motivates me every day to be a presence for the students and adults I encounter. If I could say one thing to those in education to help them see a different perspective it would be:

That stinky kid in class that's hard to teach because you can't stomach the smell is me, that lazy kid that does nothing is me, that kid that moves in and out of the school a couple of times a year is me, that kid performing below their potential is me, that kid that doesn't have a pencil is me, that kid who doesn't care is me, that kid that has an attitude for no reason is me. That awesome teacher is me, that highly motivated highly dedicated student is me, that great mom and member of the community is me, that role model is me, and with the right people surrounding them, every kid could be me."

–Christina McDowell

Hearing this from McDowell was so disheartening. Thankfully she had someone that continued to question her potential and encouraged her to finish her education. But, what about this school that failed her? The teachers let her shrink until she disappeared and did not graduate from school. Notice how in middle school it was okay for her to do nothing as long as she did well on her tests. Where is the accountability, where is the teacher stretching her to become a stronger student, what about the guidance counselor inquiring about her attendance? This should never have happened to this Black girl.

Growing up in school I was that Black girl that tried to be everybody's mama. I wanted all the Black girls to succeed. I wanted all the girls to see that using profanity is not cute. Fighting, even though I got in a tussle or two of my own, is not cute. Laying down with whoever comes your way is not cute. Playing the dumb girl role so that some boy can feel smart, when you are brilliant, is not cute. And I tried to be as non-judgmental as possible at all times knowing that we all have our flaws, me being the first to raise my hand and admit that I was far from perfect and no angel.

We all have our days where it gets hard. It gets frustrating and we want to give up and we lose ourselves and we act out of character. We have to learn to reflect, redirect ourselves, grow, and do better the next time. But some girls like the ones that are going to be discussed in this next chapter are some hard cases to crack. But even the highest wall can fall, even the highest mountain crumble all in due time.

6. Trying to "De-Ratchetize" Black Girls

I am still trying to face the fact that sometimes, it is what it is. As a woman that has been a young Black girl, grew up with young Black girls, raised a young Black girl, and taught young Black girls...I had to come to terms that I and we cannot save them all. This is not to say that when the going gets tough or when the "sugar honey ice tea" hits the fan that we simply give up. Sometimes we have to find other means or a more creative way to approach them.

Some Black girls have layers upon layers of issues that require so much work to peel back that it may take more time than you have to get through. Our girls are only with us for a limited time. For me, I did not get my girls until high school initially and up until then some of them had been completely and utterly ratcheted and had no intentions of me or whoever else changing that.

Now getting to the "it is what it is," let me be plain, some of this ratchetness is inherited from mom, grandma, or even auntie. And I can admit at 36 years old, I still have a ratchet moment or two. To clarify, by no means am I asking anyone to not be themselves, please …do you booboo, okay. However, being fully aware of who you are, embracing all side of yourself, and know when to utilize your complex parts is vital to your success in school, your career, and your life. I love to laugh and have fun, take risks, and enjoy life, but knowing when to bring the ratchetness out of your tool belt is an art that must be mastered. We have to learn it is okay to express ourselves but know our audience.

Your friends should be approached differently than your classroom teachers, and your parents, church member, etc. They are all different audiences and receive things you say in very different ways.

Some girls have no desire to be other than what makes them comfortable. They are not going to conform in any way, shape, or form. They are raw and uncut and will tell it like it is. Behaviors that have been learned from a young age from family, friends, and sometimes reality television (Parents you do have control over this, just saying). A fragile mind without guidance can confuse negative behaviors as being the norm and follow them. Knowing "my mama will come up here and cuss you out", or advocate in some other inappropriate way for my negative behavior...gives a young Black girl a sense of control, arrogance, and "power" that she is willing to go to battle with any teacher or adult who crosses her the wrong way. Many times this is a defense mechanism to save face in front of peers, but it is the only way she knows how to function...what else can you expect? They have to be taught effective ways to communicate that do not embarrass them or embarrass the adult.

This whole discussion about de-ratchetizing Black girls, I will fill you in on what ratchet in modern terms means...ratchet refers to a female with a bad attitude that does not have it together (but think that she does), she is a pure, hot mess. It comes in so many different shapes, forms, and fashions, but that should sum it up. Now, you have the young ratchet Black girl that thinks that being on public assistance is something that you should parade around and glorify and does not mind bragging about it. Do not take this the wrong way. Not at all. I have had to get public assistance. I've known family members that had to have public assistance, but public assistance is just what it's called, it's assistance to help you get back on your feet. Not a place that you should continuously have to stay in. This dependency can be somewhat another form of slavery, keeping Black women at a disadvantage.

We have to get to a point where we are leaving legacies for our children Black women. Where we are showing them how to build wealth and not staying in governmental bondage. It gets to the point where it seems like you just cannot get out of it. Now, there are some parents with specific situations and some elderly people that are in need and will continue to have that need due to different circumstances, so they may require long-term help. However, if you are in good health and have a sound mind there is no reason you cannot find some way to go out and hustle and grind to either further your education, become some sort of entrepreneur, or find some skill that you are good at so that you can build wealth for your family.

It breaks my heart to hear young Black girls come to school talking about when they get their food stamps. Stating how income tax time is the second Christmas. For one, that is not anybody's business and whether your mom cares if you share that information or not, does not matter. Some things should just be kept private.

What Is Not Understood, Needs to Be Said

I have been on home visits with some of these same young Black girls who like to brag and talk about those sort of things in school, but when I show up at their home, they have a look of shame on their faces because they lived in public housing or things may not be as warm and fuzzy as they put on. It fascinates me how some of these girls know how to work the system before they even get to high school or get out of high school and need to know how to use the system themselves.

Dr. Leake is not judging where you come from. Dr. Leake knows very well where you come from and where you are going to have to go to get yourself out of it. She has been there. We must learn how to have some respect for ourselves, respect for our situations, and a plan so that we do not stay there. Some people may or may not agree with this, some people make be offended, but it is the truth. And even if some women do not want better for themselves or feel they cannot do better because of the circumstances...want better for their children.

Tomboy ratchet Black girls. This is a girl that may be very insecure about the way she looks. She may have found some solace hanging out with the boys. They make her feel welcome. They make her feel wanted, but they are also not after what she's got between her legs. These boys allow her to be herself without any judgment. This is something that she does not get from the girls who talk about her because of her clothes, hair, hygiene, or physical features.

This young lady is no one to play with, she is ready to rumble with any man, woman, boy, or girl that comes at her the wrong way. She likes to fight, she's rough. She is slick with her mouth and could care less about what you think at this point. I know with young ladies like this sometimes parents and the teachers find it hard to breakthrough, but it is possible. I have seen some of the biggest and meanest, you know what they call themselves, breakdown and cry. They do not feel loved. They do not feel like they get the attention from their parents or their siblings at home. These Black girls feel like they have been placed in a box by their teachers. As a result, they find shelter where they feel most comfortable and they build up defense mechanisms for those that try to interfere with their process.

Do not be mistaken, a lot of times these young ladies are very smart, brilliant even. They are resourceful and have a lot of street smarts. They hide the fact that they are intelligent. Instead, these Black girls can get negative attention by acting up as a clown or as a bully, they show out in the classroom, at home, on the playground, or anywhere else they may hang out. They do this to gain clout from their "friends" who may only be around for entertainment purposes or they are afraid of her as well.

One thing you have to be sensitive about is, you have got to let a girl be who she's going to be. Let her know there's always a positive way to maintain their identity, while also keeping a sense of self with their friends and their family.

It's a balance. And I know some of this comes with life experiences, but we have to make sure that we intentionally place people in our young Black girl's lives that can guide them. This can prevent them from getting to the point where they have dug themselves into a hole that they cannot get out of.

Then you have those that are wannabes, they want to be ratchet, but they're not very good at it. These girls come from very prominent well-to-do families but also put on a front. They try to act like they're "quote-on-quote" from the hood to fit in. They use more slang than the girls from the projects. They bring more drama to accentuate their otherwise dull lives and to cover up the fact that they don't have to act the way that they do. These girls are followers.

These young Black girls have people at home that care about them, but they decide to put all of that to the side. They pretend that they are "down", and sometimes sacrifice their grades, their behavioral records, their attendance, and their future because of it. These girls try to become the company that they keep. We have to give them the confidence they need to know that being smart does not equate to being white. Being smart does not equate to being better. Having a stable home is not a crime, as long as you do not look down on others because they do not have what you have. Count your blessings. If you are a smart Black girl use that power to help other young Black girls. Once again, we have to be in this together. We cannot do this without one another.

I have come across girls that are not ratchet at all, but they have the mother, of all mothers, of ratchetness. This is a hard one, because as Black women it is difficult for us to have the conversations that we need to have with each other about helping raise our young Black girls. No one wants to be told anything. "You can't tell me how to raise my kids. You're not paying any bills. You're not putting clothes on their backs." And so on and so on. We have to be able to put our pride aside long enough to figure out what is right and what is best for our young Black girls.

When they say it takes a village, they were not lying. That is the whole truth and nothing but the truth. The Covid-19 pandemic has been more than a testament to that. The number of calls received because parents were tired of their children being at home because they couldn't handle, it's astounding. The social media posts, memes, and out-pours for help have brought a new R-E-S-P-E-C-T for educators. Parents found out that the struggle is real in the classroom.

7. Middle School Can be a Game Changer

There is something that happens between the innocence of elementary school and the reality of high school that can change the course of education and life for Black girls...middle school. The transition from being in the cozy comforts of your classroom with your cubby, friends, and sweet elementary teacher to the confusion of having to change classes, teachers, lockers, increased workload, and the combining of several elementary 5th grade classes to form one new 6th grade class can be overwhelming. You go from being the big dogs in the 5th grade to starting at the bottom of the barrel in 6th grade and the increased competition of finding your place amongst all the new students from surrounding elementary schools can cause stress and anxiety.

What is it about three to five different elementary schools coming together? All of these friendships clashing into one cesspool. When you compound this with puberty, hormones, and being Black and female you can have a heap of trouble on your hands. Our girls are placed in the lion's den and have to navigate through all of these emotions and challenges. During my time as an educator in middle school, I have seen our girls fall out of love with reading and education. Some young Black girls were sweet, had all satisfactory on their report cards, and high marks once they started getting letter grades, and in some cases were the teacher's pet. These young Black girls get to middle school and all of a sudden, they have something to prove. Because who wants to be on the receiving end of being bullied? So, to avoid that I'm just going to be the bully. Young Black girls go from eager to please primary school girls to these hormonal, preteen divas that are trying to figure out who they are. They are trying to find their niche and battle all of these obstacles at the same time.

Some Black girls also have to deal with struggles that follow them from elementary to middle school or the grade level they just left. This is what some of the Black girls are walking into: You have a track record following you. You do not get a clean slate instead, you get the murmurings of the teachers that had you before who did not know what to do with you. You have learned from previous mistakes over the summer and you've become more mature ready for a fresh start, and you still do not get a second chance because your reputation proceeds you.

Some Black girls will get along just fine. They may have been labeled AIG or as having good behavior. So, they get placed in certain classes with fewer distractions, but then you put all the students that have issues in one class and expect them to be able to learn? Please tell me on what planet does this make sense? Where instead of learning they're in the world competing with who is dressed the best, whose hair is the best, who has the newest Jordan's? Are their nails done? Who has the newest cell phone? And they are completely obsessed with social media.

The new bullying is now done via social media. You can be a complete bad, you know what, behind a cell phone. On Snapchat, Instagram, Twitter, Facebook, and YouTube videos as well. You can curse somebody out from miles away. The video spreads around the school, and all of a sudden there are rumors of fights, he said she said, and everything else in between. I cannot tell you how many fights, counseling sessions, suspensions, and friendships could have been saved had social media not been involved.

These girls are recording themselves fighting and record themselves calling out each other's names. Exposing one another, it is completely and utterly toxic. We have to teach them that there are better alternatives to resolving issues and confronting each other than the use of social media.

Parents if your young Black girl has a cell phone...check that girl's phone. There is no such thing as privacy for a middle school girl. There should not be anything going on, in that phone that you are not aware of. Save her now so you are not getting her out of something later. She may be mad, but she will be grateful later she had someone in her corner who cared enough to protect her from herself. If you have built a relationship with your daughter she will eventually understand that you are looking out for her best interest.

Somehow, once they reach high school, a lot of Black girls regain their love for education and the desire to become more and do more with their lives. Reality hits and they began to think about their futures when they get to high school. However, it can get to a point where they are so far behind it takes them until their junior or senior year to get caught up and their GPA has suffered and is not where they need to be to have the choices they should have to be successful.

We must create stronger foundations in the home and initiate effective and sustainable programming during Black girl's middle school years. We have to find a way to keep their eyes on the prize. This program has to specifically target Black girls and provide enrichment activities and self-exploration. Some ideas could be finance, health, hygiene, mental health, career exploration beyond just the normal college track, etiquette, and most of all the importance of education and the opportunities it brings.

8. We Should Not Have to Conform to Survive

Essentially Black women are 3-dimensional people. If you are a Black female you already have an understanding of this. Being able to conform depending upon who you are in the presence of. I do not consider this to be fake. This is tactfully knowing how to cater to your audience if you have to. I know when I need to have a professional conversation, a mama conversation, a firm conversation where constructive criticism may be involved, and conversations with my family and friends. At all times I am always me.

This can be a process that can take time to adapt to depending on the situation of the girl, or it's something that just comes naturally and can happen fairly quickly. For example, in the first grade, I was identified as AIG. Back then they just called it (AG) academically gifted. So, throughout my elementary career, at certain times I was taken out of the classroom and place with a smaller group of students that had also been identified and I was the only Black female. At the time there were two other African-American males within the group, so I did not feel you know any different. But going into Middle School and High School, even those numbers began to dwindle to the point where I was the only Black student in the classroom.

This may not seem like much to some, but when you're a young Black girl you can find yourself in situations where you have to prove your Blackness to some, while at the same time proving you belong in the classes you are in to others. You deal with nicknames like "white girl". Comments from others saying "You think you are white?" "Do you think you're better than everyone else?" "Why do you talk that way?" "How come you in all those classes with all those white people?" And then in the classroom, everyone looks to the single Black individual anytime anything that has to do with race comes up. Or when you are reading *Huckleberry Finn,* and we have to skip over the n- word. "Yeah, you better not say it", I would say to myself. Also, reading books like *Roll of Thunder Hear My Cry.* They looked for you as the gauge for how to respond or what they should or should not say. Let's not forget to use my opinion to determine how all Black people feel, which you cannot do.

Some white and non-black talk out of the side of their necks. "Oh, you don't act like the other Black girls. You're not as ghetto as the other Black girls." To be perfectly honest in my years of education there are equally as many white girls that are just as ratchet as Black girls. Dealing with the scrutiny of trying to balance your classmates and your school friends can be exhausting. I will not generalize because some of my white friends do get it, but some did not. Why should any Black girl have to choose between the two?

How can the white girls say that I'm their friend when I don't get invited to the birthday parties? I don't get invited to come over after school. If it doesn't have anything to do with the classroom, we don't have any conversations. Please do not count me as your friend when in reality, I do not count. We are just associates that have been placed in the same classroom for the semester.

Not all white people have these misconceptions of Black girls, but it can still be tough when you're the only one present in the classroom. You have to constantly battle with the conversations that can come along with being a young Black girl in an all-white classroom. The questions about your hair. "Oh, how did your hair get that long? It was just this length last week." Please do not act like white girls do not wear hair extensions, fake ponytails, clip-ins you name it? The weave is created equal.

Dealing with the misconception that: if you are smart that it is equivalent to being white, if you take honors or AP courses you are being white, if you speak a certain way and enunciate your words, you are trying to be white. Why does everything that has to do with something positive have to be associated with being white? And to be honest, there are several other students, young Black girls in particular, that should have been in the same classes that I was in, but somehow along the way, they were overlooked because of the way they looked, the way they talked, and the way they acted. Because when testing for what is now called AIG, there are a whole lot more ways to qualify than just looking at pure standardized tests and grades.

Academically gifted does not mean that you're smarter than everyone else. It just means you learn a different way. That is something that a lot of parents need to look into and advocate for their children. And a lot of teachers need to take it a step further and measure student's ability not by just how they act, but what they are capable of doing. Christina Rose, Culture Coach, M.Ed. discusses her encounters with this issue:

"As a young girl, early as five years of age, I vividly remember being called *uppity*, *stuck-up*, a *goody-two shoes*, and someone who was *"actin' White"*. This continued throughout elementary, middle, and high school. In college, however, things shifted. Perhaps, it was the like-mindedness of those who, too, shared my experiences. I never imagined that those experiences from those earlier days would find a way to seep into my adulthood, forcing me to sacrifice my self-worth to fit into the boxes and structures that would ultimately invade my peace and freedom, and in some cases, attack my sanity.

It has been an overwhelming journey to not be Black enough for my beautiful Black people. And, it has been unnerving to constantly "check myself" in White spaces. My livelihood is tied to a White space, and for years I find myself wrestling with ghosts from my youth. One day, I felt it was too much to bear. And, the process of becoming authentically and unapologetically black, I began with my hair, a decision that forced me to deal with what it truly means to operate in freedom.

Cutting my hair to return to my natural state was more than a movement. It was me accepting what I felt was a tugging at my soul. I was seemingly walking in this newfound freedom, and I remember going to school wearing my twist out. Students gasped, "Oh my gawd, Mrs. Rose, you cut all that hair." However, it was my White colleague who I saw walking down the hall who left me somewhat speechless. *"Oh my goodness, Mrs. Rose. I had no idea who you were walking down the hall. Your hair...it's just so different and cool; it looks like little snakes are coming out of the top of your head."* - Behind the smile, I bit my comeback. She continued by asking me if she could touch it because it looked so soft. I respond with, "No, my hair is sacred, and I only allow my stylist and my man to touch it."

And, last year, I attended a top-notch education conference, alongside several colleagues. Naturally, I gravitated to a familiar face, and we conversed about so many things. The conversation shifted, and she said, "I did not know how to take you. You always seem a little boogie and stuck-up. But girl, you're up in here with a Hillman T-shirt and twists. You need to work on becoming a little more refined." So I asked her if I should look like it was Easter Sunday in the 80s? She laughed it off as I internally cried for her. At that moment, I realized she was battling the ghosts I dealt with so long ago. She was shrinking herself, failing to walk in her authority and freedom.

Education, as diverse as it is, when it comes to students, falls within a White space. White leaders have judged me, and I am certain it starts with my hair. For some white educators, I wonder why it's so hard for my work to speak for itself. Why is it so hard to focus on my consistent results? Is my successful track record with students, parents, and the community not enough? A former leader did not think I had the look which I assumed was that *uppity, stuck-up,* a *goody-two shoes,* and someone who was *"actin' White" type of look.* This leader was determined to replace me with what she deemed more appropriate until she stopped to realize my value to her regime. It was already too late; I recognized her broken core. Together, we could have achieved so much, but that would have required me to shrink, and I'm beyond that now. "

–Christina Rose, M.Ed.

No girl of any color, race, sexuality, background, etc. should have to wrestle with an identity crisis at such a young age. Why do Black girls not get the freedom to be themselves? Why are we constantly questioned about EVERYTHING we do? Not just by white people, but by other Black people. We are in an endless battle to try and please everyone except ourselves. Once you allow these Black girls to come into their own, make their own decisions, and inspire them to see what they can become this is when the magic starts to happen.

Unfortunately, some of us (Black women) do not tap into this magic until later in life due to what we have had to overcome in our childhood and Black girlhood.

9. Finding Black Girl Magic

"The most disrespected person in America is the Black woman. The most unprotected person in America is the Black woman. The most neglected person in America is the Black woman." —Malcolm X

If only I had known then about myself what I know now. It sounds cliché, but in this case it is very true. If I had known I could fly at an earlier age because I had my wings, I cannot even imagine where I would be now. I have managed to recover from some of the trauma I have endured as a Black female. It has been years of holding my tongue and thoughts to myself. Refusing to comment on the outlandish things that have been said to me and asked of me. Being told by my guidance counselor that I was better off going to a community college. Being told that I was too loud in my various roles as an educator. Tirelessly worrying about my Blackness being too much or in other cases not enough. The list can go on and on. It took me "coming into myself" to realize my strengths and my truths as a Black woman.

Some parents depend on the school system to raise their young Black girls until that young Black girl does something wrong and the parent wants to blame the school, the teacher, and everyone else but the child or themselves for the problem. We have to be accountable. We all have to be accountable. I'll be the first to admit if I've done something wrong and I will try my best to correct it. I believe in giving our young Black girls second chances, or third chances if needed, because some need more than others, but everything is handled on a case-by-case basis and it takes more for them. We have to have more than just the school on board. Everyone has to do their part. All right, let me take off my administrator hat before I get completely off-topic.

I made a vow to touch as many as I can touch, save as many as I can save, and do all that I can do while I'm able to do it. We cannot get bogged down by the ones that we do not save, but we can have victory in everyone that we do save. Live with ourselves knowing that we gave it an honest try for those that may not have had a chance if we were not present in their lives.

In the quote by Malcolm X that opens this chapter, he refers to how the Black woman is the most disrespected, the most unprotected, and the most neglected person in America. And he is telling the truth. The struggles I've seen my mother endure, my grandmother endure, my peers and colleagues, and even my own daughter endure brings tears to my eyes. Being looked over for scholarships, job opportunities, advancements, mortgages, and even getting a car. Not getting that role in the play or not even having a role that a

Black woman or Black girl could even partake in to begin with.

We have to put ourselves in positions to help even the playing field for our young Black girls. We have to have that seat at the table. It is one thing to rally outside the doors, but it's another to be in the building, in the seat at the table, making the decisions. But until we protect ourselves, until we respect ourselves, and until we make sure that our offspring and our fellow Black women are not neglected, we are going to find ourselves staying at the bottom of the totem pole.

The bottom of the totem pole has to be strong to hold everyone else up, but we have to find a way to get to the top. Our presence is needed. Our presence is needed everywhere, not just in music videos, reality television shows, and social media. We have to make ourselves present where young Black girls are waiting on someone that looks like them to show up.

What Is Not Understood, Needs to Be Said

We have made wonderful strides over the years in modeling, fashion, sports, entertainment, healthcare, military and most of all politics, but please keep in mind that education is the foundation. No matter what, every young Black girl has to go to school.

When I accidentally became a teacher. Yes, I do say accidentally because I had no intentions of it, but God had other plans. I wanted to make sure, with every ounce of my being, that every Black girl that came my way, or Asian, or Hispanic, even some of the white ones who felt like they were outcasts, had a place to belong. Which is not always the case. We spend so much time trying to find a place to belong, but there's not always something created for us.

So, when I walked into that high school in the fall of 2007, I was told that the Black girls were at the bottom academically, with graduation rates, behavior, you name it. (And just a sidebar, there was a Black Queen Educator in my interview that grilled me, but was advocating for me and aided in my being chosen for my first teaching assignment. I love you, Mrs. Pratt). With this information at hand, I initiated the step team, as well as a spin-off of a club that I was a part of in Middle School, which was called the I'm a G.I.R.L. Club. When I was in middle school, this club was run by a fabulous Black woman, and it did allow us to have some fun experiences as young women. I initiated the IAG club, as the girls called it, and used modeling as the foundation just to give them some activity, but it was surrounded by both the importance of Education, Health/Hygiene, Building self-esteem, self -respect, and lifting one another. I know that all girls do not desire to be models, so there were opportunities for those girls to help with wardrobe, sound, music, advertising, organizing events, and fundraising.

We did small activities like having a Mary Kay consultant come in and give some makeovers to some of the girls that we knew normally wouldn't wear makeup or were insecure about themselves. We performed at community events with the YMCA and local businesses. We did shopping trips. We did college tours. We went to other schools for programs. We did things for Black history. We gave back to our community with different drives and clothing collections. We did a yearly fundraiser where we put on a show that showcased all the girls and the things that they had learned and done. And in three years it made all the difference.

These girls were going off to college, the military, law enforcement, and the medical field. They were excelling inside the classroom and outside of the classroom. The disciplinary records dropped and their achievement levels went up. And Black girls were no longer at the bottom.

Now part of my philosophy was every Black girl cannot or does not want be an athlete. Not all Black girls want to be cheerleaders. But that does not mean they can't be leaders. You have to give them the outlet and the opportunity that they need to be able to see beyond themselves.

To be perfectly honest, I had no idea of what the outcome was going to be. I just wanted to give the girls something to do. It did have a purpose and I think that purpose was met. In the next chapter, you will see that all of the efforts put in have resounded with these young ladies well into their adulthood and they're even sharing some of the same practices with their daughters today. There were many more participants and the club was diverse, however; it targeted Black girls. So, please take time out to read those testimonials from these young women.

Let's not get it twisted, some of these girls came from very strong families. Some had a lot of people in their corner and some did not. However, just having that extra push, that extra outlet, that individual in their lives that was not going to judge them right or wrong, as family, sometimes tend to do, and provide ongoing, consistent support, they were able to rise above their circumstances. They rose above the small town that they came from and went out into the world and begin making their imprint.

When people talk about Black girl magic this is what they mean. This was magical, and it has taken me all this time to realize it. Once again, I just wanted to make sure Black girls were not at the bottom because there is room for us all at the top.

10. Testimonials from former IAG Members:

What Black Presence In Schools Can Do

Cynthia Brooks M.A. in Human and Social

Services, Teacher and Case Manager, Age 30

Growing up I was always the "only Black girl" which did wonders on my confidence...and not in a good way. It wasn't until high school when I joined a new club called IAG "I'm A Girl" that I truly started to learn about and embrace self-love. I can remember the feeling I got walking...no strutting across that stage hearing my teammates and the audience scream my name. It was a confidence booster for sure. But it was more than just that.

The coach, Mrs. Leake formerly Ms. Green was a big part of why I even joined in the first place. It was such a breath of fresh air to see someone who looked like me and carried herself with such grace and fashion. Ms. Green was one of those teachers who listened and didn't judge. I can distinctly find out I was pregnant at 19 after I went off to college going to visit her at the high school with a few of my best friends and telling her I was pregnant. She was the only adult in my life who didn't shame me, her only words were "well okay...how are you feeling? What do you need?" Little does she know that conversation changed something in me. I took a year off to care for my little one then got back on my Bachelor's degree.

I graduated with my BA in Child Development and in 2020 with my MA in Human Social Services. My dream is to help at risk youth to build confidence and be a part of the foundation from which they grow...just like Mrs. Leake did for me.

Jordan Shankle Naval Lieutenant, Physician Assistant, Age 29

As a Black woman in society, with a desire to make a change, to be heard, to be seen - even without being seen; where do you start? You start within yourself. But how? Initially, there is familial support, friends, or your internal desire to overcome the odds and touch success.

So, how do you measure success? How do you obtain it? The answer is through experience. What and who you experience in your primitive years help develop you as a person. As children, we often spend or have spent most of our time in school. Five days a week; for 8hrs per day. Our influence is there; our motivation and drive are there. However, what if you never see anyone who looks like you?

I can vividly remember my 10th grade year in high school when I saw a beautiful, African American woman preparing her classroom for the new school year. I was immediately intrigued by her presence, her style, her intelligence, and her keen appreciation for education. I was hoping and praying to be placed in her classroom; solely because she looked like me – unaware that she would be the staple of change in my life forever.

Mrs. Leake immediately established comradery amongst young females during my high school years. The principals and core values of each organization she created, such as IAG and our school step team, seeded character and developed my self-esteem.

What Is Not Understood, Needs to Be Said

My experience with a Black female educator developed a unique perspective and understanding of my place in society. The educational benefits of having someone who understood me on a different level established a sense of belonging and it helped reduce self-limitations in regards to how far I can succeed.

To revert to my prior question. How do you succeed? How did I succeed? How did I become a Naval Lieutenant, serving my nation as a Physician Assistant? How was I able to handle the rigor of combat medicine while deployed to Africa, Spain, Italy, and Portugal? How was I able to receive the esteemed Naval Accommodation Award and Humanitarian Medal? It was seeing someone who looked like me. It was someone who closed an educational gap and fostered self-confidence. It was the love instilled; the words of encouragement. It was a Black female teacher empowering me to look beyond societal stereotypes; to touch the depths of who I am to transcend the best version of myself — to the world. I am thankful. I am appreciative.

Pachia S. Lee, Account Manager, Age 29

Thank you for the opportunity to share my experience as a member of the I'm A G.I.R.L. Club program – the modeling troop that forever changed the trajectory of my life. Looking from the outside in, many questioned the purpose and intent of the organization, but I knew it was going to be a game-changer.

The program was the starting point of my journey in developing self-love, care, respect, awareness, and confidence as a maturing, young lady. In an environment, where everyone and everything can seem so vain and unfair, the program was my haven for inclusion and acceptance. It played a major role in helping me to overcome many challenges during my last two years in high school.

More importantly, it became my creative outlet; a safe space to building me and stretching me to be the best version of myself. Here is where I learned to walk with boldness, speak with conviction, and dream big. The most astounding thing is so many of those values and standards that we were taught then still uphold in my life today. Looking back, I can proudly say the program was genuinely dedicated to empowering girls.

Thank you for being the difference, Mrs. Leake.

Cynthia J. Baldwin, Navy, Certified Registered Dental Hygienist, Age 29

When I think back to my time spent growing up in a super small town with very few opportunities for girls who looked like me, I am forever thankful for being a member of IAG and the Step Team at South Stanly High. I didn't see my first Black female educator until I was in high school, and I often wonder how I would have turned out without the mentorship of Tempest Leake. This was my first time having a Black female who wasn't related to my care and invest in my future. I think of the confidence that this organization instilled in me right now as I sit as the only female in a majority male run clinic, I don't shy away from giving my opinion nor am I ashamed of my intelligence and gifts.

Granted, I always knew that I planned to join the Navy after I graduated high school, I was amazed to see a woman the same color as me with a degree in science and teaching in the field as well, this influenced me to pursue my education while serving in the Navy, on top of my military decorations I am also a Certified Registered Dental Hygienist. I met Tempest when I was 15 years old, now as I sit here as a 28 year old woman, about a month away from giving birth to my first daughter I plan to instill in her all of the wonderful characteristics of being a gifted, intelligent, respectable lady as she grows.

Shanequa Clark, Income Maintenance Caseworker II at DSS, Age 28

I am pretty sure I can write more personal experiences so I may add on to my portion. But I want to say thank you for all you have instilled in me and for believing in my potential more than I did at times.

IAG and the step team MADE my high school experience. High school had its challenges itself, but those 2 extra-curricular activities let me "be me". Ms. Green then, now Mrs. Leake, challenged us to be better, gave us an outlet to express ourselves through fashion, modeling, dancing, making lifetime memories, and principles to take on with our adult lives. Gifted Intelligent Respectful Ladies, still ring in my head as I now have a daughter. I honestly wish we could still have that reunion!

At South, there were little to no Black female or male influencers and educators so I cherished the ones I did have because it showed the representation that I needed and still feel is lacking but on the rise in this small county. I still have some of the best memories from looking at CD's and pictures from our performances. Going down memory lane and saying I participated in a CIAA step show and PLACED as I attend the step shows and activities as an HBCU student/graduate makes me feel proud. I am thankful for the heart Mrs. Leake has, pouring into young girls who may have struggled to find their way, have that big sister who they could look up to, or just being surrounded by the love they longed for.

Still watching your accomplishments and still inspired to keep going and being a better role model to younger girls. I am a graduate of the illustrious Winston Salem State University where I majored and graduated Cum Laude in Social Work. I am still working on my graduate degree in Social Work and plan to go back and finish soon. I am currently working at Anson County Department of Social Services as an Income Maintenance Caseworker. I have a beautiful 5-year-old daughter who amazes me every day and sees so much of myself in her.

Liakayla Davis, Medical Assistant, Age 29

 Both IAG and the step team had a big impact on my life. Before IAG I had never worn heels. I just did not have the confidence to do so because I'm already tall. Being In IAG gave me so much confidence and helped me out with my self-esteem. It helped me to realize that everyone is different and we are all unique in our own way.

The step team was more fun than anything, just being able to be a part of the team and have fun and love it was a big thing for me. I will forever be grateful for Black educators, especially you, because not only did you teach us so much you were always an outlet for us. You motivated us so much as young Black girls in the environment we were in. You are still a big motivator to us to this day! I have an Associate's Degree in Applied Health Science as Medical Assistant. I work at the hospital as an HCT (health care tech) and I'm currently applying to get into the nursing program.

Thank you for everything you have done for me and for inspiring me to never give up!

Shenea Dumas, Detention Officer, age 27

Hey, Mrs. Leake joining IAG taught me to have more confidence in myself instead of depending on someone else to tell me who I am. You had a lot of patience with me, with me being such a tomboy! (Still a little) but I don't mind wearing those heels instead of tennis shoes all because of you! You helped me soooo much and I loved it I just pray my daughter has a chance to grow up being educated by a strong Black woman like you! I can truly say in you and Ms. Pratt's class I had high grades for them to be science classes!

Still, until this day I tell my son physical science is my favorite! I pray you're doing well and continue to pave the way because we're watching and following. Oh, yea my career in Law Enforcement will be my 6th year come October. Just a different role I just started at Stanly County Jail as a Detention Officer. I will be going for my basic law enforcement come September of this year.

Scotesia Dunlap, EMT, B.S. in Public Health, M.S. in Physiology, age 29

First and foremost, I just want to congratulate you on all your success and the ones ahead of you as well. You changed our outlook on life and motivated us especially the young Black females more than you will ever know. We were lucky enough to have one Black educator than to be blessed with a second one with your phenomenal personality was even more profound! You took the high school to a different level for us!! I was never really a girly female, but you made walking in heels enjoyable and fun allowing me to express a different side of me. I am forever grateful for all the knowledge, wisdom, and lessons learned from you! I have a BS in Public Health and MS in Physiology. I am currently an EMT and can work to build patient contact hours so I can advance in the medical field. At the end of the day, you were my motivation to continue to push forward and never give up on my goals.

High School Responses 2011

Kyera McClendon, Music Major, Accounting Minor, Age 26

This year, 2011-12 will be my second year being in I.A.G. I love I'm A G.I.R.L. It helps me better communicate with my friends and it's a time for us to come together and have fun, having friendships is important to me. I love all the girls in the club and I respect every one of them and I will continue to respect them. We get to come together and learn more about one another, our community, and the things we can do to improve our community starting with ourselves, it makes me happy because these are the things I occupy my time with. I'd like to think that if I wouldn't have started I.A.G. I wouldn't know some of the things I know today. For example, when the lady from the health department came to talk to us about sexually transmitted diseases, I learned a lot. Mrs. Leake, you always mediate with us and taught us valuable lessons. You teach us self-respect, and how to carry ourselves as young ladies. I can't wait to see what this year will bring. I hope there is no drama and I hope all the girls get along. I also look forward to exploring my options with colleges and our first show. I enjoy the responsibility of being in the I.A.G. Club.

As a senior, I hope my last year is filled with leadership and I will set an example for the younger girls. I hope to learn more from the club because I'm pretty sure I haven't learned all there is to learn. We have a lot of goals to achieve as young ladies and we can achieve them together through the club. I enjoy having a support system in the club and also with the step team. It helps me direct my energies toward something I enjoy and I'm grateful to have that. I don't know where I would be given the opportunities and the enlightenment of the club. Maybe somewhere failing classes? I don't know, but since I'm not I'm proud of myself and what the club has helped me with. That's the reason I'm happy to

be a part of the I'm a G.I.RL. Club. I love you, Mrs.
Leake

Quinesha Carter, Restaurant Manager, Age 26

The I'm A G.I.R.L. Club has changed my life in a lot of

different ways, the G.I.R.L. stands for gifted, intelligent, respectful, ladies. I believe throughout the years I have become those things. In the I.A.G. club we learn how to dance, model, and have fun but it's not all the dancing and modeling, we have also learned how to be strong and we realize we can be whoever and whatever we want to be in life as long as we make the right choices. As long as I have been in the I.A.G. Club I've learned how to carry myself as a young lady. The club has taken college trips to learn more about what college is like so the I.A.G. club deals with education as well. Since I've been in the club I've also learned how to let some things go and get along with others that I didn't get along with before...I hope all of the younger girls enjoy this year and the same to all the

girls that would like to be in I.A.G. in the future because it will change their life.

Deneisha Smith, Phlebotomist, Age 27

I have been in I'm A G.I.R.L. since I was in the 9th grade. And since then we have been on many trips and helped people. Being in I'm A G.I.R.L. not only let me do the one thing I love doing, but it has also helped me connect with my mother and helped me learn how to talk to her. I'm A G.I.R.L. has been a big part of my life in so many ways, like when we went to the beach and Mrs. Leake gave us a packet with papers in it for our parents. My mom read those papers and we tried some of those things. We have had toy drives for the needy and it made me feel very good to bring the toys or clothes in when it was time for the drives.

Summary

To understand us, is to know us. This book is part of the steps it will take to help you get to know us. Until society understands the obstacles that Black girls face there will not be change. We as Black women are trying to climb our way to the top despite the stumbling blocks that are in our way. There is a difference between equality and equity. There is a difference between being tolerated and being accepted. We need more than the same thing that everyone else is being given. Black girls need more than just to be tolerated and passed on. Accept us for who we are and provide the means to assure equity can be achieved.

Look at where we come from historically. We spent centuries in bondage here in America, we spent decades waiting for rights that Black men and white women received first. We toiled years as nothing but nannies, housekeepers, cooks, and bodies to be used for whatever the case may have been. This is not something that goes away overnight. These issues have to be addressed head on to get the results our girls deserve.

I charge you today to make a difference in a young Black girl's life. And if you are a young Black girl I challenge you to challenge yourself. Look deep within and discover your beauty, your intelligence, your purpose. I also charge you to lift up your sisters along the way. And pay it forward. If no one else helps us, we have to help ourselves. Free us from the bondage we place on ourselves and the bondage we allow others to have over us.

References

Cai, Jinghong. (2020). National School Board Association, https://nsba.org/Perspectives/2020/black-students-condition-education

Daniel, Nicole. Oct. 8, 2020 'A Battle for the Souls of Black Girls'. *New York Times.* https://www.nytimes.com/2020/10/01/us/politics/black-girls-school-discipline.html

DRESS CODED: Black Girls, Bodies, and Bias in D.C. Schools. (2018). https://nwlc.org/press-releases/dress-codes-hurt-learning-for-black-girls-in-d-c-new-nwlc-report-finds/. April 24, 2018

Epstein, Rebecca; Blake, Jamila J.; Gonzalez, Thalia. (2017). *Girlhood Interrupted: The Erasure of Black Girls' Childhood.*

Mental Health America. Black and African American Communities and Mental Health. Mhanational.org/issues/black-and-african-american-communities-and-mental-health, 202

ABOUT THE AUTHOR

 Tempest Green Leake, Ed.D., is a wife, mother of three, author, coach, and educator. This North Carolina native has spent 14 years in education. Her career in education includes being a science teacher, instructional facilitator, testing coordinator, and currently an assistant principal. Dr. Leake is passionate about the education and fair treatment of black girls, especially in rural areas. She has devoted her time to mentoring, coaching, and guiding young Black girls to being the best version of themselves.

Please visit: glycwithdrleake.com for more information

Email: glycwithdrleake@outlook.com

Made in the USA
Middletown, DE
18 April 2022